Crypto for Beginners

How Cryptocurrency and

Blockchain will change the world

Giovanni Casagrande

All right reserved. No part of this book may be reproduced, stored in a retrieval system, or transmitted in any form or by any means, without prior written permission of the publisher, except in the case if brief quotations embedded in critical articles or reviews.

Every effort has been made in the preparation of this book to ensure the accuracy of the information presented. However, the information contained in this book is sold without warranty, either express or implied. Neither the author, nor GC Publishing or its dealers and distributors, will be held liable for any damages caused or alleged to have been caused directly or indirectly by this book.

GC Publishing has endeavored to provide trademark information about all of the companies and products mentioned in this book by the appropriate use of capitals. However, GC cannot guarantee the accuracy of this information.

Editors: Giovanni Casagrande

Graphics: Carlotta Cisterni

First published: December 2018

Production reference: 1290318

ISBN: 9781791844387

Published by Giovanni Casagrande

giovannicasagrande.com

About the author

I'm Giovanni Casagrande, a known name in the world of cryptocurrency. I am an Italian who has well over 20 years in the cryptocurrency industry. I am also an Economist from the best Italian Universities, with a passion for marketing and growth hacking tactics for the development of different projects and programs.

Fortunately, I lived in this transition and equipped with the two decades of the traditional experience of business experience which is now being coupled with new decentralization industry market skills.

My passion has expanded in the cryptocurrency industry. This has seen me invest my talent and skill into being part of the team growing this industry.

Also, I have vast experience being in the cryptocurrency field as an advisor to a lot of programs. Well over 60 successful and booming programs in the cryptocurrency world have my signature on them. Projects like Fidelity House, Avinoc, FortFC, Farm2Kitchen, Xera, Securix, etc. to mention a few.

With blockchain and the advantages attached to it, we can do a lot and different things. Things that were not possible before with old technology.

Table of Contents

Chapter 1 - This book 1

Cryptocurrency & ICO - terminology 2

Chapter 2 - The very basics of Cryptocurrency 3

What is cryptocurrency? 3

What are Smart Contracts? 4

The concept of money 5

Money as construct of authority 6

Money as a language 6

Evolution of Cryptocurrency.. 7

How to use and invest in Cryptocurrency 10

What is a Cryptocurrency Wallet? 11

What is a Cryptocurrency Exchange? 13

How Cryptocurrency Works 13

Investing In Cryptocurrency 14

Why Should I Invest In and Use Cryptocurrency? 16

Up-To-Date Crypto Regulations 17

The Eminence of Blockchain 18

The Rise of Altcoins 19

Decide Which Coin Catches Your Interest......................... 22

Invest the Right Amount 24

Crypto Secrets 26

When Can We Use Cryptocurrency 34

Chapter 3 - The modern way to seed funding 37

What is ICO? 37

How to Promote ICO 41

ICO yesterday and ICO today 43

Chapter 4 - Understanding blockchain and its application 45

BLOCKCHAIN 45

Blockchain and DLT 48

Distributed Ledger Technology 49

BLOCKCHAIN 49

BLOCKCHAIN TECHNOLOGY USE CASES 50

Tokenization 52

Chapter 5 - The Story of Bitcoin and Altcoins 57

Bitcoin and Altcoins 59

Various Types of Cryptocurrencies and How They Work 60

Altcoins 62

Cryptocurrency Success Stories 66

Introduction

About this section

In this first section, we will introduce the topic of this book. In addition to that, we will give a short introduction to general Cryptocurrency and ICO. This beginner guide to ICO and Cryptocurrency is useful for understanding the remainder of this book.

Chapter 1
This book

There is still one item on financial times that everyone wants to see before they wrap up their financial forecast for the day. Cryptocurrency has become the buzzword in the world today. While it is surrounded with so many controversies ranging from its volatile nature, the amount of uncertainty that has made it trump all other events to record the biggest theft of all time - all happened in this space... the potential it holds cannot be overruled. And the question still echoes will cryptocurrency ever moon again? If we decide to neglect every other factor that would sound like speculation, such as the recent use of cryptocurrency to sign players in Italia FL, the news surrounding ETF, and Wall Street, and many others, we cannot but agree that the invention that powers cryptocurrency has come to stay, Blockchain technology. And many big corporation are already in active research to understand many ways they could utilize blockchain in their respective businesses. Amazon, Walmart, Microsoft, Samsung, and a host of others are actively using and experimenting with Blockchain technology. It remains to wake one day and see that each of these organizations have created a utility token to power their invention - this is possible anytime, and a reason you should conclude on your consideration, study and invest in this space as it remains the future of money and everything.

This book covers the most important topic of cryptocurrency and ICO, with light shed on the background technology, blockchain with all in combination to help you understand what the future will look like and what should your stake in be in the near future.

Content of this book

This book is divided into five sections. The section can be read in the order you like, but the most logical order is to begin from section 1 and stop reading after you've finished section 5. The information is non-technical and can be read by anyone who has a cryptocurrency wallet or hoping to get one, a cryptocurrency investor or one hoping to invest, a cryptocurrency trader or one hoping to trade, and those who seek to understand the concept of cryptocurrency and ICO including ICO project managers.

In this book, we will attempt to cover the basics but also provide more in depth information on every topic. For advanced readers, some basic information will be common knowledge and could be skipped altogether.

In this first section, we will give some background information about cryptocurrency, what it is, how to invest in it as well as the best time to invest in it. To help you understand what cryptocurrency is, we will take a dive into the concept of money and then return to the development of cryptocurrency.

Cryptocurrency & ICO - terminology

In this book, we will often write "cryptocurrency" as Bitcoin and sometimes as it is. Of course Bitcoin is just one content type of cryptocurrency. There are many other cryptocurrency such as Ripple, Ethereum, and many others which are generally called altcoins, and since Bitcoin dominates all, we will in some case use Bitcoin to mean cryptocurrency. ICO means Initial Coin Offering, and will also be used in sections relating to ICO in this book.

Chapter 2

The very basics of Cryptocurrency

This Chapter

In this second section, we will introduce you to the very basis of cryptocurrency. We will cover a broad definition of cryptocurrency, where we will look out for what protocols are cryptocurrency hinged on. We will discuss the prevalent two protocol, the proof-of-work, and the proof-of-stake protocol. From there, we will progress to discussing on what a smart contract is - this will cover many definitions and take us back to history when Nick Szabo first had same like the concept as the smart contract. In defining smart contract, we will also capture the novel definition of Ethereum's founder, Vitalik which will take us to the concept of money. The concept of money will be an attempt to take us through various school of thought on money - this will help you understand this book's standpoint as well as help you make your takeaway on the concept of money. That will take us to the evolution of money where you will get to understand the cycle of cryptocurrency - where it is currently in its development stage, some hurdles it has passed through, milestones - including major hacks and government regulations. Thereafter we will discuss on how you can invest in cryptocurrency - where you will get to know the difference between a cryptocurrency wallet and the conventional bank account; how to invest in cryptocurrency and more. We hope you'll find this chapter interesting!

What is cryptocurrency?

Cryptocurrency can be defined as a digital currency that operate outside a central protocol. Cryptocurrency transactions are validated and controlled through an encryption technique that are solved in consensus. To validate a cryptocurrency transaction, each request to transact is broadcasted throughout the network known as nodes, who will in agreement decide to validate or nullify any transaction. The specific governance protocol adopted by Bitcoin is Proof of Work (POW) while some altcoins uses Proof of Stake (POS). The process that guides and ensure that every action within the network is incorruptible is known as smart contract.

What are Smart Contracts?

Smart contracts are self-executing contracts. They are set of conditions expressed in code that runs on the blockchain that independently facilitate, and verify transactions. A smart contract could be any form of computer program that enables the foregoing. The concept was first coined by a computer scientist and cryptographer, Nick Szabo known for his research in digital contract in 1994. Recently, the concept has been popularized with the advent of blockchain technology or distributed ledger. Blockchain technology makes the concept practically possible because it's immutable (meaning records cannot be altered once deployed). This helps to make sure that once a code is deployed, it will not be altered. Although with development in technology codes in smart contracts can now be altered but in a way that irregularity is almost impossible.

The Wikipedia Encyclopedia defines smart contract as "a computer protocol intended to digitally facilitate, verify, or enforce the negotiation or performance of a contract. Smart contract allow the performance of credible transactions without third parties." Another definition of a smart contract that should be considered is that of Vitalik. According to him, smart contract occurs when an asset or currency is transferred into a program…

> "and the program runs this code and at some point it automatically validates a condition and it automatically determines whether the asset should go to one person or back to the other person, or

whether it should be immediately refunded to the person who sent it or some combination thereof" Vitalik Buterin - Ethereum

Bitcoin has a fairly short history, with an anonymous creator preferred to be known with the pseudonym, Satoshi Nakamoto. It's an invention created on January 3rd, 2009 with the aim to create a digital currency that is self-executing through a timestamp hashing-based proof-of-work protocol. According to the Bitcoin whitepaper, relying on a financial institution to solve the problem of double spending was an unending approach, and one that required the user to (at their expense) trust a financial institution in order to make financial transaction possible. Trusting an institution eliminate the benefit of digital signature. Rather than trust an institution, the problem of double spending can be solved with a peer-to-peer protocol. The peer-to-peer protocol utilizes a time-stamp method to hash each transaction into an ongoing chain of hash-based proof-of-work, forming a record that cannot be changed without redoing the proof-of-work. Bitcoin can be adequately conceptualized as a protocol, and this will lead us to the next discourse, what is money?

The concept of money

You probably are familiar with the concept of how money evolved to become what it is today.

Money as Value

Google defines money as "a current medium of exchange in the form of coins and banknotes or coins and banknote collectively." while this definition of money can be true, some of the properties of money as contained in this definition will form our discussion later in this chapter. Properties like banknotes, current medium of exchange, and coins collectively. On the other hand, the Wikipedia encyclopedia define money as "any item or verifiable record that is generally accepted as payment for goods and services and repayment of debts in a particular country or socio-economic context." This definition of money is somehow close to what money is than Google's definition. In that, it includes certain elements such as, an item (not necessarily a banknote), verifiable record, generally accepted (not dictated), as payment for goods and services, in a particular country. This definition of money is encompassing and would have made us settle here but it also raised certain issues that we need to look into if other concept of money would address them. Concerns such as generally accepted as oppose to government accepted, and/or an item etcetera etcetera. Something becomes a thing of value when people of certain race, jurisdiction or nationhood decides that it should be of value to them. In that case having a sort of money where only a section of these individuals become the ones deciding on behalf of others is somehow disturbing and a thing that has made the problem of money lingered for so long. Let's take a look at other concept of money.

Money as construct of authority

Money as we know it (banknotes) comes from central authority and is part of the reason we have generally see money as a construct of authority. It's conventional to see that every independent state has it at their beck that a construct of authority in the form of money is necessary to get the sovereign nature that nationhood demands. And because the government, as the authority, they can easily maneuver money to get the will of the people whichever way they want.

Money as a language

According to Andreas Antonopoulos, author of the Internet of Money, money is a language human beings use to express value to each other. According to him, language is a social construct that enables human to exceed what he calls "the don bond number." He defines it as the total amount of number required to form a kinship. That for money to be used across a particular kin, the users of money forms a particular bond that's exclusively preserved to those of the kin. In other words, money is a common language that forms a kinship through which exchange of value and asset between themselves becomes possible even without a third party.

Money as Control

Money can also be seen as a system of control, in that it gives power to those who are at the helm of affair of controlling how users spend money. Government is also a conventional pioneer of money as a means of control. Something irregular with money as control is that it enables those at the helm of affairs to use this control to their favor.

Money as a content type

Money is also seen as a content type. Such money is possible only in the era of distributed ledger. When money is sent and received on a flat network, it's regarded as a content type. Money as content type is also regarded as data that can be transmitted over the internet. A typical example of money as a content type is Bitcoin. Bitcoin is the protocol or cryptocurrency that represents money as a content type on the blockchain, without a client and a server but with contributors and volunteers who cannot attack the system. Volunteers run Bitcoin as a peer-to-peer network of nodes that validates transaction through a hashing proof-of-work protocol. Money as a content type is the future of money where the issue of double spending is resolved without having users to trust a central authority for them to successfully conclude a financial transaction.

Evolution of Cryptocurrency

Bitcoin as the first operational cryptocurrency could be regarded as a result of an evolution of several other attempt geared towards creating an anonymous distributed cash system. Exemplary yet short-lived outcomes of these efforts were B-Money and Bit God's proposal by Wei Dai, which was referenced in Satoshi's work. These currencies were formulated but they were never developed. Part of this sheds light to the popular belief that Satoshi Nakamoto may not be one person, that it may very well be a group of people. Since Bitcoin was first introduced as a paper posted to a mailing list discussion on cryptography, the real identity of these brains behind the act till today remains a mystery. It was in 2009 that the Bitcoin software was made available to the public for the first time, alongside mining, which is the process through which new digital currencies are created and transactions recorded as well as verified on the blockchain network. At first, it was impossible to assign monetary value to the emerging units of Bitcoin since it was yet sold or bought.

However, in 2010, 10,000 unit of Bitcoin was equated to $10 when 10,000 units were swapped for two pizzas. An amount which is today worth over $100m. Shortly after then, the price began to increase to $1,000. Thereafter the increasing price of Bitcoin began to decline in value leaving a lot of people who had at the point invested their money in Bitcoin suffered loss, when the price plummeted to about $300. Still at the time, it was believed that the price of Bitcoin would take upto half a decade before it would rise again to $1,000. Till date, controversy surrounding Bitcoin was as a result of numerous loss that made people of limited knowledge about the protocol to often refer to it as "scam". And perhaps it may be as a result of criminal activity by people who sought to take advantage of the fact that Bitcoin was designed with anonymity and lack of control. In 2010, Bitcoin hacks and theft became the order of the day, which led to an exposure of a major vulnerability in the system. The situation of Bitcoin at the time was problematic as the Bitcoin developer, Jeff Garzik noted. It was the biggest hack of all time when Bitcoin lost 184 billion BTC to hackers. Later on, in 2010, when Bitcoin had its inaugural sales, with the aim of attaching a monetary value to a unit of Bitcoin for the first time. It was in 2011 that rival digital coins began emerging in their numbers. With the debut of these new industry players, Bitcoin began receiving a lot of criticism after claims emerged that the currency is being used on the so-called "dark web", especially on notorious sites such as Silk

Road. In what was a proof that no publicity at all is bad publicity, the monetary value attached to Bitcoin began taking an upheaval before crashing back down. In 2012, Bitcoin enters popular consciousness, including an imaginary trial in the third season of US drama titled The Good Wife, entitled Bitcoin for Dummies. 2013 saw a failure to agree for Bitcoin – a time in which a new rule of transactions refused to suffice from the conglomeration of the currency's holders. This culminated in a Bitcoin fork, which entailed the blockchain literally splitting into two. For six hours, there was a duo of networks operating at the same time, with two different transaction history version, which led to an unavoidable drop in the value of the cryptocurrency.

As the story of Bitcoin began getting a lot of suspense, people began to tap into the whole idea of distributed ledger, inventing alternative digital currencies that could extend the use case of Bitcoin – all of which are known as altcoin. These coins were built to have at least one characteristic of Bitcoin, and develop it to the fullest. Some of them offer greater transaction speed, better anonymity and some recent others priding in scalability to mention but a few such as Ada cryptocurrency. The first two to emerge during these replications were Namecoin and Litecoin. There are currently more than 1,000 digital currencies in circulation with new ones spring day by day. So was the birth of all the valuable currencies now virtually consuming a lot of space on Coin Market Cap.

The burst in cryptocurrency does not only aid in making the technology behind it better and popular each day but has also on the dark side, attracted a ton of scammers penetrating the system and getting involved in unsustainable projects that turns out to massive scam schemes as a result of the cryptocurrency boom. As a way to regulate the system, currently, various countries are putting up tight regulations that regulate how cryptocurrency crowdfunding are carried out. The first of its kind was that of Thailand, whose government placed a ban on Bitcoin, declaring that trading Bitcoin as illegal. The Ministry of Finance in Germany would not accept Bitcoin as an official currency, but rather as unit of account that paves the way for a future framework to tax Bitcoin-based transactions. In Asia, the People's Bank of China is against the use of Bitcoin at all for financial transactions – a move which prompted yet another drop in the value of Bitcoin. Against all odds, the first Bitcoin ATM was launched in Vancouver, Canada in 2013.

From 2016 till now, Bitcoin and Altcoins began to head mainstream. Testament to this acclamation was in the number of Bitcoin ATMs, rising from around 500 at the beginning of the year to barely under 900 by the end of it. In the same year, Uber in Argentina switched to Bitcoin payments, and the national railway and software website Steam in Switzerland became one of the users that accept the digital currency. Then, the DAO (decentralized autonomous organisation) was founded in May of the same year to be a stateless venture capital fund on the Ethereum blockchain and the largest crowdfunded project to date. But this establishment was hacked by unknown users only after a month of its launching, recording a third of its entire assets being siphoned.

How to use and invest in Cryptocurrency

To invest in cryptocurrency, you have to know how to initiate a transaction with cryptocurrency.

How to Use Cryptocurrency

Cryptocurrency can be put to use in a number of ways, but knowledge on how to use comes at a premium. Trading and investments remain the most common use-cases of cryptocurrencies (meaning, you don't own Bitcoin for the sake of holding it but for the sake that it amount to some unit of valuable asset-data that you can trade for anything of value you want), and here is how to go about it.

To get started with using cryptocurrency for trade, it is of paramount that you understand what a wallet is, as well as an exchange rate, as they would be useful to trade efficiently. Once that is achieved, it generally becomes a stroll - not much different from filling out a form and waiting for the transaction to be processed, provided your information can be verified by the exchange of your choosing. In other words, you need just two things to use cryptocurrency; a cryptocurrency wallet and a cryptocurrency exchange to trade on.

What is a Cryptocurrency Wallet?

A cryptocurrency wallet is a software program used in storing private and public keys with which you can use to interact with your digital assets on various blockchain. A wallet helps you send and receive digital currency from your device to another device with a wallet address or a barcode. While some wallet would require basic information about a user to enable them to use the wallet, others don't. By mere entering your email address, a wallet address is generated from which a private and public key would be assigned to you. Usually users are encouraged to store their private key in a local server that doesn't require access to the internet before they can retrieve it. This is encouraged as a hedge against asset theft.

Difference between Cryptocurrency Wallet and Bank Account.

While cryptocurrency wallet communicate with the blockchain to retrieve your asset, monitor your balance, sends and receive coins from other users, it's quite different from your conventional account bank account in many ways.

1). Cryptocurrency uses a 2 of 3 Multi signature scheme to spend your asset. Part of the reason Bitcoin advocates often say it's better off to traditional banking system is because it's secured than traditional banking (especially to the users). Unlike the traditional banking system, once a bank is declared bankrupt, the users suffers with the bank. This is not so with a cryptocurrency wallet. Till now, centralized wallets and exchanges are still in operation in the cryptocurrency space yet in any case where each of these companies are declared bankrupt, the 2 of 3 multi signature protocol helps the user retrieve their Bitcoin and transfer it to another wallet or hold in on their local server. How is this possible? And as you would want to ask, if this was possible, why did we have lots of many other hack case. While hacking is inevitable, destructive hacking is near impossible on blockchain. That's why having a good knowledge of what a multi signature security is before venturing to trade cryptocurrency is paramount.

A 2 of 3 crypto wallet multi signature scheme demands that before your digital asset is spend, more than one of your private keys must be signed. And this means that to spend your Bitcoin, you and the cryptocurrency wallet company would need to sign one each of the signature for it to occur or 2 of the signature with one left for a third party (if you want) before you can spend your Bitcoin. The implication of this and as it differs from traditional spending is that, if a wallet company goes bankrupt tantamount to a bank, they cannot take over your funds because they would need to sign 2 of 3 signature assigned to each wallet (of which they have access to one), before your Bitcoin can be moved. But because you have access to two of these keys, you have the leverage to spend your Bitcoin or transfer it from the existing wallet to your local hard drive at any time you wish. This freedom is not so with our traditional banking institutions. Rather if a third party have access to your account (such as the bank or your bank account officer themselves), they can initiate any transaction with their superior signature on your account anytime they wish without even your consent - leaving users at their mercy.

2). Cryptocurrency wallet is somehow accessible like any social media account while bank accounts are not. Users can access, trade, and even move their Bitcoins from one wallet to another wallet without having to engage in ceremonies. While funds can be transferred from one bank account to another, there are however restrictions to the amount that can be transferred from a bank mobile app. This is not so with a cryptocurrency wallet. Another distinction is that cryptocurrency wallet offers users the freedom to trade themselves and withdraw at any time regardless of their trading skill. In a bank, you hardly can independently trade government stocks and bonds from your account independently.

What is a Cryptocurrency Exchange?

Cryptocurrency exchanges, are platforms that support trading of cryptocurrency for other fiat currencies or trading of altcoins for Bitcoin. The operations in platforms of this nature are not that far off from what is on offer from stock exchanges or even fiat currency exchanges in a foreign airport. And that's just about it, as the rest of this section will basically be dedicated to throwing more light on all the important things you need to know on how cryptocurrency can be used.

How Cryptocurrency Works

Generally, cryptocurrency wallets have wallet IDs, which is a lot like a bank account number, as well as security keys. Moving assets from one cryptocurrency wallet to another would involve gaining access by entering incredibly-lengthy passkeys which are the products of encryption and hash functions into the provided fields; and this is best done by copying and pasting.

Cryptocurrency wallet IDs and passkeys are generated upon creation of a cryptocurrency wallet on any chosen cryptocurrency exchange. Once access is granted into a particular wallet, transactions can be made by entering the recipient wallet address, as well as the sender's transaction passkeys in order to authenticate the transaction, and confirm the amount of cryptocurrency that is to be traded. Transactions of this nature may seem like a little bit of a hassle for those that are not really savvy with tech, but cryptocurrency usage is on the rise because of the sheer speed, boundless reach, and security of such transactions.

Cryptocurrency transactions generally take the following forms;

1. You trade and invest in cryptocurrency, i.e buy and sell.

2. You can use it as a payment option for transactions that accept cryptocurrencies of a particular kind.

3. With the help of some software, you can put together a graphics processing unit for the purpose of mining cryptocurrency.

Investing In Cryptocurrency

If investment is your preferred mode of cryptocurrency usage, and not just the regular trading (i.e buying and selling), then there exists a few options that you can explore. New crypto investors have the following options;

1. Masternode: The word, "mining", is probably one of the most popularly used word in the cryptocurrency industry. It's so popular because it helps Bitcoin infrastructure achieve its peer-to-peer consensus algorithm of POW (Proof of Work), which perhaps is the horn of the Bitcoin network. Mining is that process that helps in validating transactions and the creation of a new block on the blockchain network. Mining is for POWs as masternode is for POSs protocol. While mining requires high consumption of power, masternode on the other hand uses a staking protocol that makes validators or node owners to hold a certain amount of coin (usually referred to as collateral) so that they validate transactions with a vested interest, in a way that bad actors lose their stake at any given attack. And then they also get reward each time a new node is created. Masternodes provide the opportunity to invest in cryptocurrencies with additional benefit of earning guaranteed

extra coins while also benefiting from the increase in value that come within the cryptosphere and owning cryptocurrencies.

2. GBTC Trust. Cryptocurrency has always been regarded as something for the tech savvy and programmers however, with GBTC Trust, individuals who are casual about "cryptocurrency" can invest and trade cryptocurrency on NASDAQ.com or any public stock exchange. GBTC is a ticker symbol for The Bitcoin Investment Trust, a trust run by Grayscale that holds 175,984,800 shares of 0.00100721 Bitcoins as of February 2018 (it was 1,868,700 shares of 0.09242821 Bitcoins as of August 31, 2017, but the stock split).[1] GBTC has been the only avenue for investing in bitcoin in the open market such as stock exchange (this might change). There is also the ETCG (Ethereum Classic Investment Trust) they are some other ways you want invest in cryptocurrency with the fiat currency. You buy cryptocurrency in the market with your fiat and exchange it for fiat etcetera. GBTC trust is one the more permeable ways non-techies have often find their way profiting from cryptocurrencies.

3. Exchange: One of the benefit of trading digital currencies on exchange as opposed to other publicly traded avenues is the ability to capture any change in market at every point in time because it enables traders to trade 24/7. Even though earlier this year, NASDAQ announced their 24hr trading,[2] it only allowed for 24 hrs per day and 5 days per week. While on cryptocurrency

---

[1] Understanding The Bitcoin Investment Trust (GBTC) https://cryptocurrencyfacts.com/ understanding-the-bitcoin-investment-trust-gbtc/#citation-2

[2] E*TRADE Announces 24-Hour Trading

https://markets.businessinsider.com/news/ stocks/e-trade-announces-24-hour-trading-1016486051 exchange, trading is allowed 24/7 making them to capture the gap in market before the public market opens on Monday.

When using cryptocurrency for investment, it is advised that you be wary of the merits and demerits. But if you're looking to land a one-stop shop for direct trading and investment, then Coinbase/GDAX is easily the best bet, as it is thought to stand out from the rest on account of its ease of access and use.

Things to Keep In Mind When Using Cryptocurrency for Trade

Here are a few things you should take to heart when starting out as a user of cryptocurrency as they will guide you on how to do it successfully;

- While a cryptocurrency exchange is a lot like a regular stock exchange, never mistake both as one and the same. Exchange brokers such as Coinbase/GDAX may appear to have the same general mechanics, but there exists different specifics, as well as different entities.

Why Should I Invest In and Use Cryptocurrency?

Below are some reasons you should invest and use cryptocurrency.

Why Would You Invest in Cryptocurrency?

Cryptocurrency became a new channel for investments ever since its inception. People, having found that the value of digital currencies accumulate and appreciate over time, thought it lucrative to finally pump their funds into and wait for the day of the big catch. Crypto investors are like sand in the sea – countless. And each of them has the same goal – getting rich with minimal or no fuss. If crypto were a dead end then people would perhaps not be committing their salaries to it. Bitcoin's price fluctuations has certainly been Thor-hammering the headlines as of late. Due to this, there have been diverse discussions as to whether or not crypto is worth an investment in 2018. It's sure worth it and a major reason the crypto leftist are calling on the rightist all over for sessions to discuss cryptocurrency and blockchain. Sometimes, Bitcoin along with other digital coins undergo what we call a bounce back in value, leading to as much as a trading value of over $9000 per coin and there is a lot of speculation that the unit price is a ticking time bomb waiting to explode. With all of such news flying around and people making a fortune out of cryptocurrencies, you probably are starting to think whether or not you should join the bandwagon. This is no endorsement, but should you be looking for real-time answers, here are some reasons you probably should save up some money for crypto investments.

Up-To-Date Crypto Regulations

It is subject to argument and correction, but what can be said to be the biggest benefit emerging from the unexpected rise of digital currencies, is the fact that better crypto regulations are being introduced and now starting to take real shape. All the uncertainty associated with the system has drastically reduced because such regulations have been a significant booster for trading activities and the prices of coins subsequently. Improved targeted and obviously tighter regulations will go a long way in helping the holding of many crypto scams by the scruff and sniffing them out into oblivion. These Ponzi schemes which have previously thwarted a lot of crypto investments are now on the down-low and will continue to be, as all new currencies and investment opportunities will have to adhere strictly to certain criteria. In no time, further regulations and even the ones in existence will help quell the fears of potential investors and provide for them a more formidable foundation for prospective growth of investments.

The Eminence of Blockchain

Needful to say at this juncture is that blockchain, against all odds, is here to stay and many times its ecosystem is fully propagated when it has its own token - meaning cryptocurrency is also here to stay. Top of them all is Bitcoin which has the larger percentage of the industry and media attention on investment into digital currencies with others as alternative coins aka altcoins. Altcoins came in the light of "innovative Bitcoin" - they are mostly backed by teams that can be said and proven to be exciting and of course innovative. And then, there is the underlying technology and the powerhouse of cryptocurrencies, Blockchain, which grows in popularity by the day and is far more of an excitement than the daily fluctuations of a specific coin. Should you have the chance and will to delve deeper into the blockchain technology, you would, no doubt, discover so quickly that many global organizations are starting to pump and even ramp up investments in the form of significant funds and resources, all into cryptocurrency. These include brands such as Microsoft. Yes, you heard that right. A bit ironic and pun-filled isn't it? Microsoft investing in blockchain? A lot of brands are conducting research on how crypto could be infiltrated into their already successful business plans and strategies for the future. These moves are making further coherence on the widespread opinions that blockchain will, in no doubt become a very integral part of the way businesses will prospectively operate across the globe.

Crypto Investment Isn't Close to Rocket Science

The algorithmic replay is no job for you, so don't freak out yet – let the miners do that for you. Before the advent of digital currencies and even after, it has never been simpler to invest but something left for portfolio managers. We have heard from different crypto investors that the prospect if making the giant leap into crypto doesn't fall any short of an initial daunting experience. Some people actually need help and advice from people who have been in the business, usually at the early stages of their investments. Even in the light of alleviating initial concerns and worries, time have really changed and there is now much more information available to enable investors quickly navigate the world of digital currencies without having to deal with the many pervious barrier to entry. Coinbase, which boasts of one of the largest customer base of about 10 million investors, is one of the most popular digital wallets we know as of now. The platform allows investors to purchase Ethereum, Litecoin, Bitcoin, and Bitcoin cash but to name a few. There are also new to market investment funds such as the 10x Growth Account, a U.K- based investment platform. This opportunity recently surfaced and it allows investors to have access to a portfolio of cryptocurrencies such as Bitcoin, Ethereum and Ripple through collaboration with the Center for Citizenship Enterprise and Governance (CCEG) and their secure platform seratio-coin world. This crypto firm is in the offering of secure and easy access top crypto experts, making it the ideal place for newbies looking to invest in cryptocurrency but do not know the starting off point. With these developments and their improvements, investing in cryptocurrency has become very easy and it will get better in the days to come.

The Rise of Altcoins

The rise of altcoins cannot fall short of a reason you should invest in cryptocurrency. So far, Bitcoin has been the currency leading the way where it's from, with its domination of the crypto market which easily makes it the most recognized coin currently. Nonetheless, this does not translate into Bitcoin being the best or only opportunity for crypto investments that will worth it in today's world of cryptocurrency. It can be argued, but there is belief that the opportunity to reap the largest rewards from Bitcoin has come and gone, with those who invested in the alien coin a decade ago having made eye-watering returns. Being that the same, bitcoin fever doesn't spread as much again, the investors of today who are looking for the most promising jackpot are expanding their horizons to accommodate and invest in altcoins such as Ethereum, Litecoin and Ripple (which recently overtook Ethereum to become the second largest in market capitalization of $22.2 billion) are promising cryptocurrencies expected to prosper in the years to come. At the point we are now, it is noteworthy that such an investment comes with extremely high risks, meaning that you must be prepared to lose the entire investment. In the light of this risk, it makes it more advisable to invest at the point when you are most happy to lose, and in what is affordable. The road to becoming successful at cryptocurrency is not guaranteed, so it should only form part of a wider portfolio of varied-risk investments. Also important here is that when investing in altcoins, you should do all you can to seek independent advise before as much as making the first move on new investment decisions.

The Promising Future of Crypto

The rule of thumb of any investment is that you keep a keen eye on the long-term viability. If it happens that you become so engulfed in the short-term microanalysis, each and every variation in price will have you worrying to death that you have made the worse investment decision. So if you don't want to be caught up in that web of should haves and could haves – the list which is almost endless, you need to look at the future of the investment opportunity. Looking at the short period may cause you to panic-sell what you had invested at a higher price than you sell it for. You may rush to do this when in the real sense you can hold off until the price is recovered in full – which is the more sensible move. The crypto market is unarguably a volatile one, and the fluctuations in price will definitely happen, with some more concerning than others. The recent plummet Bitcoins has scooped, towards the $6,000 mark remaining in the bear line for about 8 months, has made even the most hardened investors a little hot under their collars. Bit recently, the price fluctuated to about $7,000 and back to the bear line of $6000+ per coin, along with seemingly bullish predictions that the price will further surge in no distant time. Because crypto has a promising future, you should always be on the lookout for investments over the medium to longer term of 1, 5 and even 10 years, because this is how people become crypto millionaires. Despite the fact that scams prevail in the system because of it anonymity, and also in the light of crypto banning by different governments, people still believe that crypto is a miracle that should be given time to fully flourish and manifest.

HOW TO INVEST IN CRYPTOCURRENCY

So you've heard about cryptocurrencies and perhaps learnt about what a gold mine it can be? Now, here's what you need to know about investing in cryptocurrencies: it doesn't come with a manual, and trust me, it's nothing close to a cake walk. If you are looking to emerge unscathed from trading cryptocurrencies in spite of the fact that it feels a lot like a Russian Roulette-esque venture, then you will need to have an edge. And the right information might just give you that edge.

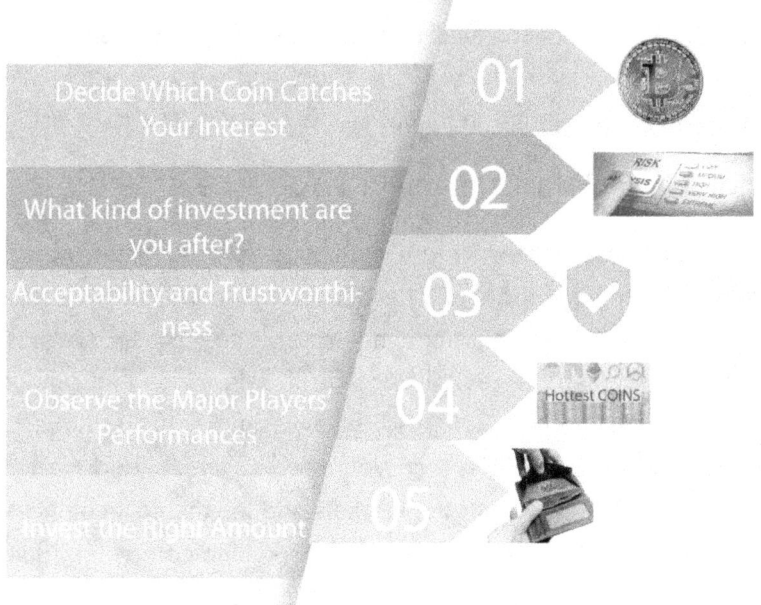

The one question on the lips of every prospective crypto investor is how much they should invest in the sector. The universe of digital currencies is susceptible to market fluctuations, partly as a result of it relative infancy. In that light, investors need to always retain that cautious attitude towards existing and prospective investments. Bearing this in mind, if you are looking to invest in cryptocurrency there are some factors you should consider.

Decide Which Coin Catches Your Interest

There are a plethora of coins in the market, and it is very important to understand the fundamentals of a digital asset, as it can play a significant role in the caliber of risk involved. Looking for the best indicator for long-term investments? Have your focus on fundamental analysis. You will need to understand how a coin or ICO functions, its history and what it brings to the table before you opt to take part in its development. The best move may be to look at the purpose of the currency you've taken interest in, how long it has stayed in the market, it market capitalization and it underling tech solutions. Cryptocurrencies that solve problems are less likely to crash compared to those that are essentially ICOs. Quick tip – the longer a virtual currency has been in the market, the more trusted it is to invest in.

What Kind Of Investment Are You After?

You will naturally want to plan first if you wish to enter the crypto market – there is no shortcut. The question then will be whether you dealing will be short-term, medium-term or long-term endeavors. This consideration is very essential because it determines that amount of money you will be committing to the investment. If you have plans to engage in regular trade, then you need to understand the market trends, the culture that drives the markets and the mentality of investors. Looking to go further? Study up on the market indicators, fundamental and technical analyses, incoming market-moving events, general tech news as well and developer announcements. These among many other variables should be the next step in upping your game.

Acceptability and Trustworthiness

As in most regular markets, trust is a crucial element in crypto investments for prospects. In order for someone to put their money into a cryptocurrency or ICO project, the person must have through one process or the other conclude that they can trust the idea enough to invest in it. in the world of virtual currencies, this process can be predicated on the three key factors about new tech billionaire philanthropist and entrepreneur Peter Thiel has discussed. This include a unique idea that offers tangible solutions, an incremental improvement (which need a good development team) and the capacity to coordinate complex ideas. In the real sense, these three points are the best indicators for a long-term investor. In the Economic Club of New York in March, there was a talk during which Peter Thiel analyzed the trustworthiness of digital currencies by means of drawn parallels between Bitcoin and gold. Both assets are considered as stored of value in their own way, are not backed by the government, have inherent values that remain unclear and most of all are immutable in different ways.

Observe the Major Players' Performances

It doesn't matter the field which you are in – learning from the knowledge of predecessors is always a good employ. Crypto is no an exception. As a matter of fact, taking a look at the major crypto players so far might be more important due to the volatile nature of the market. Any small mistake can cost a fortune or crash down your entire holdings. What is regarded to be the commonest maxim among crypt investors and finance experts alike is that you should only invest your money when you are willing to lose it. Putting that into perspective, it translates into a low percentage of your net worth. 'Do they really do as they say?' is the big question. A man such as Erik Finman, who is a crypto millionaire, for instance invested $1,000 in virtual currency when he was 12 years old. He had just little cash, yet went on to risk it – a high-reward process that had earned him millions. At a point, Jeremy Gardener invested a larger portion of his stock holdings in crypto, and since then he has become a millionaire. At the end of the day, these investors took giants leaps to invest in crypto, and they have made it thus far. More importantly, these folks were ready to lose the money no matter how much.

Invest the Right Amount

With the advice that you should only invest the amount of money that you are ready to let go as in a gamble, the right amount may be up to you. This rule of thumb is nigh on impeccable. If it is till vague or somewhat superficial to you, think about it in a different way. You wake up one fateful morning with all your investments in shambles. Would it then make you unable to pay your bills in the next month? If it does, then you are definitely investing too much. As a matter of fact, any kind of investment, whether legit or gamble-like, should not swallow up all your savings. The money you are investing, if it is lost, will always hurt. But if you take time out to do the investments properly, it won't be as devastating one if the worst comes to pass. Investors should always ensure that they maintain 95 percent of their investments in a well-diversified portfolio across a variety of asset classes, sectors and geographical locales. This will help position investors to mitigate risks and take advantage of opportunities as they come up. For starters, you can start at around 5 percent of your portfolio in crypto because it is believed that there are no more doubts that virtual coins in some form are the future of money.

The biggest motivation for the use of cryptocurrency is the edge it has over fiat currencies in terms of its borderless nature, its secure (if you take the best practice), and it helps you keep your financial transaction private. In other words, cryptocurrency transactions are known to be highly secure while providing a reasonable degree of anonymity to the transacting parties. Also, cryptocurrency transactions are immutable, meaning that they cannot be altered or changed - making double spending almost impossible.

Cryptocurrencies are used mostly because there is no chance of faking or reversing transactions. And more to it is the elimination of third party in transaction - making transaction cheaper with less friction of forex regulations. Cryptocurrency transactions attract little or no fees which makes them ideal and reliable when it comes to quick and easy cross-border trade, unlike regular currencies. More so, by virtue of their decentralized technology feature, they are generally available to anyone and data is stored with all users. No central servers exist, so there is no talk of hacking and even when a bug exist as common in the early stage such as.

Cryptocurrencies are currently being accepted as a means of payment on a number of platforms. ATMs that are designed for cryptocurrency transactions are also being used in some parts of the world. And here is another interesting point; history was made some few weeks ago when cryptocurrencies were exclusively used in the purchase of an Italian professional football club.

Cryptocurrency market is known to have witnessed something of a sudden boom in recent times on account of the increasing acceptance, and this can be construed to imply that there exists the possibility of small investments transforming into large sums within a short time.

Cryptocurrency boom has created a sort of scrambling on professionals and amateur speculators in a bid to get in the act by profiting from it. This has sparked investment in Bitcoin and altcoins with a view to making quick returns or bolstering investment portfolio. This forms another motivation for using Bitcoin, as it affords the opportunity of making substantial returns on investment.

But just like any other investment, it is not without risks. Investors in cryptocurrencies are best advised to be wary of the market's instability and volatility. In as much as it holds the potential to bring in fortunes, it could also prove costly if things go south.

Crypto Secrets

There are some things that do not get discussed nearly enough when it comes to the subject of investing in cryptocurrencies and you might get caught up in something of an elephant project or a wild goose chase if you go in blind-sided.

Knowing the underlying mechanisms and intricate details which govern investments in cryptocurrency is very essential as it often prove the difference between success and failure in the venture. Suffice it to say that investing in cryptocurrencies can either help you rake in a fortune or reduce you to penury, but if you are furnished with the knowledge of how to go about it, then the former is the most likely outcome.

That said, this section is focused on helping you scale and grow your cryptocurrency portfolio by arming you with the right mix of tools with which you can succeed. There is a plethora of content out there when it comes to cryptocurrencies. Hardly a day goes by without some new literature being put out there with regard to the subject. And in the midst of all the melee and bedlam created by the muddled details, it might be hard to sift out the grain from all the chaff.

But to ensure that a number is not done on you by information of the bogus kind, you might want to avail yourself of reliable information and give yourself the best possible chance at succeeding. And that is what this section is dedicated to. Together, we shall walk through some of the best kept secrets when it comes to investing in cryptocurrencies. This guide is basically aimed at exposing some of the less-often-talked-about strategies which govern investments in the venture - not the relentlessly drummed up narrative on the lip of every crypto enthusiast and even observers that has become obsolete, banal, and somewhat clichéd. Now, let's examine what I would like to refer to as some of the most up-to-date information and strategies which govern cryptocurrency investments which you have probably never come across before now.

- Diversification Does Sound Like A No-Brainer But It Is Not Always The Right Move

I'm pretty sure most crypto enthusiast and so-called "experts" will come at me with rocks and pellets for holding such an unpopular opinion, but trust me, it takes nothing away from the fact that there is sense and truth in that assertion.

Virtually every corner of the crypto web you look at and every crypto egghead you seek counsel from will urge you to invest in multiple cryptocurrencies and not overly commit yourself to one type of coin. This would actually seem like a very reasonable advice if we were talking about any other asset or investment but crypto.

We are here now, and we are talking crypto. So I'm going to say that it is not always a good idea to diversify with crypto. Trying your hand in different cryptocurrencies can only be advised if you are looking to buy more coins with a view to increasing the volumes of coins in your possession for more profitable gains in the future.

Essentially, it is important that you figure out what holds the most value for your portfolio and then stake only as much as you can risk losing in a single investment. The amount invested should only be something you can live with in the event of a loss. It might be true that spreading your portfolio across a range of coins can minimize your risk of suffering losses at all, but that only further echoes why you must only proceed with investments whose value is something that you can afford to lose if things go south. A strategy of this nature which revolves around implementing diversification for the purpose of triggering more investments in cryptocurrencies could do a solid to your overall profit.

But it is not all that straightforward and not exactly as black and white as it may come across at first glance. Be wary of pitfalls in the form of the price fluctuations which are kind of rife in the crypto market. It is not uncommon to see coins take a severe hit and lose as much as 40% of their value in a single day; an occurrence that might yet make a case for the proponents and advocates of diversification.

On a similar note, another caveat lies in the difficulties associated with identifying which coins are the real cash cows, which ones will flatter to deceive, and which ones are just there to make up the numbers. Cryptocurrencies are bound to always seem like a highly-speculative venture for the foreseeable future regardless of how robust an investment portfolio is deemed to be. It is important to note that fixating on the ups and downs that seem to occur on a daily basis will do little to improve the situation but looking at the big picture might supply that glimmer of hope which is enshrouded in the fact that the crypto market cap will only continue to go up, and that might supply all the motivation that is required to exchange those fiat currencies for virtual tokens.

- Price Is Never More Important Than Market Cap

Earning some short-term gains is not exactly the same as following a proven strategy, and that's kind of one of the misconceptions held by most crypto traders. Tales of astonishing success and incredible fortunes built on the backs of crypto, which are made waves or are still making rounds around crypto circles, are largely borne out of a bullish stance on altcoins and a handful of lucky trades. It is also somewhat interesting to note that such apparent fortune-yielding moves were made when prices of the coins were below $1, and purchase was easy due to their relatively low prices.

Now, here's an interesting bit; relevance is attached to the coin price factor only after consideration has been given to the total supply. The metric that holds the most relevance and significance is the number of coins in existence multiplied by the price of those coins in the market, as this gives an idea of the market capitalization of that particular crypto asset.

Paying attention to such details as comparing the total market cap of a particular cryptocurrency with how many of them you are buying will afford insight on the scarcity, supply, and long-term value of that cryptocurrency are factors you should give consideration to when buying a particular cryptocurrency.

An illustration that could serve to buttress this point could be cited in an individual who invested $10,000 in, say, Litecoin, whose market cap were subsequently increased by 20%. A profit of $2,000 would have been made on the investment, which is not exactly far off from what would have been garnered from a coin with smaller market cap that had witnesses a shift in its value.

In any case, it might seem like wishful thinking to have a coin with a larger market cap experience a jump to a value that is higher than that with small market cap. The point that is being driven home is overly fixating on coin price is not ideal as it is largely a function of the total amount of tokens in circulation, which sort of renders it an unreliable point of reference when it comes to investments. When next you shop for altcoins, the best practice would be to keep an eye on those with a relatively low market capitalization.

- Don't Give Too Much Importance To The Absolute Price Of A Cryptocurrency

When investing in cryptocurrencies, the three essential ideas to pay attention to is that past performance does not necessarily give an accurate indication of future potential, the sunk cost fallacy, and to seek out positive future value. These three ideas are founded on the ideals of leaving intact the proceeds from the investments which make up your crypto portfolio.

As a matter of fact, there exists only few instances in which collecting the money earned from your investments could be considered as justified and these instances are mostly hinged on changes in market circumstance. There exists the possibility that there has been changes in the amount that you are worth and perhaps a large amount of high risk cryptocurrencies are in your possession. In any case, it is always advisable to have only between 10% and 20% of your disposable income steeped in this sort of investment. Anything more would seem like over-commitment.

Withdrawing the earnings of crypto investments can also be justified in such cases where the future of a particular cryptocurrency begins to be enshrouded in doubt and looks bleak at best, or if you are looking to leverage your finances for other purposes.

Essentially, there is always the option of relieving yourself of your portfolio if it works better with your peace of mind. This is especially a good idea if you have amassed considerable fortune through intelligent investments as it would appear you are just fiddling with "house money" that seems unreal. But the caveat that you should be wary about in this approach is that going about crypto investments in this manner can just spell the beginning of some pretty bad decisions since the mindset that the funds are not really theirs in the first place begins to creep in – which is basically the scourge and bane of gamblers.

Another reason to withdraw your earnings is if you lose faith in the future of cryptocurrencies, or think that your money could be utilized elsewhere.

One final point is that you might decide to pull out from your portfolio if it will improve your peace of mind. This could be a good idea if you have earned a large amount of money through investing intelligently, as you are now playing with "house money" that doesn't seem real. Investing in this state can lead to some bad decisions since some people rationalize that the funds were not theirs to begin with, which is the slippery slope that gamblers face.

- Being Right As Often As Possible Is Not Exactly The Goal

Getting egos involved in the decision-making process is actually one of the bigger problems associated with the crypto community. In crypto dealings, you must be mindful of the fine line that exists between being right and making profitable decisions -- because these two points are not exactly buddies who are always found in the company of one another. Fair enough, there exists some sort of primordial need to be right inside virtually all of us, there a kind of satisfaction that is derived from being right. But if the goal is to rake in a substantial amount of funds in the long run, then you might be better served finding loopholes in events instead of being overly concerned with being right all the time.

- Both USD And BTC Should Be Given Consideration When Measuring Crypto Worth

Don't just go about building castles in the air with regard to the valuation of the amount of crypto in your possession. Attention must be given to other currencies and you must juxtapose them with your crypto asset to ascertain how they stack up to Bitcoin in the long haul. The wise move is always to make trading moves that will have a net positive effect on the value of your BTC.

This doesn't necessarily imply that you should restrict yourself to trading only Bitcoin, but the idea is more like beef up the value of your portfolio by considering its value in BTC. A stagnant or diminishing BTC valuation might be suggestive that buying and holding on to your crypto assets might just be the best way to go.

- Buying Low And Selling High Sounds Good But It's Not So Easy

Buying cryptocurrencies while they are on the cheap and selling the moment they reach their peak is something that is one the lips of virtually every crypto expert out there. In fact, personally, I feel like I am going to gag or throw up the next time I hear those lines.

However, what quite few of them will tell you is that is buying on the cheap and selling at the peak is one hell of a task in reality -- it is actually a lot harder than most people care to give it credit for. The volatility and uncertainty which are prevalent in the cryptocurrency market can make it several geometric progressions harder to see beyond the values and peaks. This problem is also somewhat echoed by short-term price fluctuations, as well as the largely speculative nature of the market.

Playing the long game often proves a profitable move in such a circumstance. This entails retaining possession of your crypto assets for a long periods as opposed to making small gains over shorter periods, which takes a lot of courage and will. But if done right and with precision, it could prove a far more profitable path to tread than selling based on hype which can blur your foresight and reduce your chances of identifying the best time to buy and sell.

- Don't Invest More Than 20% Of Your Income In Cryptocurrencies

It would be a terrible misjudgment on your part when it comes down to making crypto investments. By way of financial advisory, not more than 20% of your total income should be tied up in cryptocurrencies. Unlike other investments, this is not exactly a case of "the bigger the risk, the bigger the reward." Here it's more like: "the larger you invest, the larger you risk losing." And it doesn't help much that most people only have between 10-20% of their monthly income left after offsetting bills.

Splitting one's left-over earnings into two halves and investing either half in both Bitcoin and Ethereum does sound like a plan. This can serve get you in on the act and help you grab your won slice of the crypto pie without overly putting your finances at risk.

- Surround Yourself With The Players In The Industry, Not Family And Friends

It is not uncommon to have people venture into the crypto game, hauling along friends and family. But be that as it might, such a move might not exactly do your chances that much good. The reason for this is connected to the fact that, at the moment, there is a lot of instability, volatility, and uncertainty bedeviling the existence of cryptocurrencies.

There are really no assurances and no safe havens as nothing is really set in stone. Dragging friends and family into the game comes with the burden of bearing the brunt if it happens that things go south, and you don't want to be that guy.

The other downside is that you might inadvertently assume the position of "family crypto expert" and get bamboozled with a barrage of calls and questions from friends and family bordering on investment advice. And if things go wrong on your call, it's going to be on you. Even if no one actually gets to flat-out say it, they are all going to thinking it, and you don't want to be carrying that kind of weight on your shoulder.

If family and friends do show interest, you will be better served by encouraging to do some digging by themselves about the potentials of the asset and the dangers there in. On your own part, you need to surround yourself with individuals who are a step ahead of you in the crypto game as this will enable you sharpen your investment skills, impart you with a keen eye for a gold mine, and improve your judgment. The goal is to grow in the game and you can only do this by leveraging the skills of those that have been there and done that instead of depleting what rudimentary knowledge you have managed to build.

Other details to keep in mind when dealing with cryptocurrencies are summarized as follows;

- Read about cryptocurrencies every day.
- Always do your research.
- Think long-term.
- Invest responsibly.
- Do not call it quits with your day job under any circumstance.

When Can We Use Cryptocurrency

Cryptocurrency can be put to use in normal, everyday transactions, as well as trading. Bitcoin can be traded on market exchanges for altcoins or altcoins for Bitcoin. There are thousands of altcoins on the market exchange but you've got your work cut out for you in the area of finding out which ones to trade. It is also possible for individuals to trade cryptocurrencies between themselves based on pre-established agreements.

More so, there are a lot of platforms and establishments where Bitcoin are accepted as a means of payment

Best time to invest in Cryptocurrency

Often people ask, 'when is the best time to invest in cryptocurrency'? This typical freshman question has often been accompanied with a rule-of-the-thumb answer: 'invest in the dip'. Relational to the psychology of a market cycle above, for every investment portfolio, hopes are high when the prices for a potentially valuable investment are low. And there is almost no better point in the history of cryptocurrency as it is now where the worse is over with cryptocurrency. The major bans, restriction, and all worse situation are getting off of cryptocurrency. Google recently (at the time of this book) lifted their initial ban placed on cryptocurrency ads on the world's largest search engine. Recall

THE VERY BASICS OF CRYPTOCURRENCY

that in June this year when the initial ban was placed by Google, it sent the price of bitcoin down by 10%. Relieving cryptocurrency off this ban is tantamount to a 10% equivalence ROI for every investment today. That is one, many other indications are rolling out and the prediction of an extremely bullish market situation on bitcoin to the sum of $96,000 is around the corner and should serve as enough incentive that now is the best time to invest.

Another way to examine the best time to invest, is to look back at historical moments at investing. 1990 - 2000 for example recorded an all-time tech boom in history, and imagining someone who had invested from 1990 to 1998, they could still have made money.

> Every pullback - no matter how steep or how long - was followed by higher highs. I expect the same to be true in crypto for many years to come. - Palm Beach Research Group

Cryptocurrency is barely a decade old, meaning it is still within its infancy stage, and hopes are high about this industry. Let's take a look at the volatility history of bitcoin since 2011.

HISTORY of BITCOIN
since 2011

2011	2012	2013
Down 94% June-November 2011 from $32 to $2	Down 43% June 2012 from $7 to $4	Down 80% April 2013 from $266 to $54

2015	2017	2018
Down 85% November 2013-January 2015 from $1,166 to $170	Down 40% September 2017 from $5,000 to $2,972	Down 61% January 2018 from $19,206 to $7,500

"

- Down 94% June–November 2011 from $32 to $2

- Down 43% June 2012 from $7 to $4

- Down 80% April 2013 from $266 to $54

- Down 85% November 2013–January 2015 from $1,166 to $170

- Down 40% September 2017 from $5,000 to $2,972

- Down 61% January 2018 from $19,206 to $7,500

"

Bitcoin as many other investment portfolio has its own high and low - even though bitcoin is yet to be categorized as a stable currency, it still worth your investment especially in its low times as this. As you can see from the infographic above, people who bought at its dip benefited significantly - even if you might want to assume that it would stabilize at this point, do not also forget the predicted bullion run of bitcoin in few years from now. Doing your own research and investing out of conviction would remain your best advice.

Chapter 3

The modern way to seed funding

This Chapter

In this chapter, we will take a look at the prevalent means blockchain-based projects generate funds for the development of their infrastructure and tokens. We will specifically look at what an ICO (Initial Coin Offering) is, its origin, how it grew to become a generally accepted means to seed funding for blockchain-based projects. We will also take a look at some recent development in ICOs especially with VCs' (Venture Capitalists) interest succeeding in persuading blockchain-based project to mitigate the risk often characterized with the industry by issuing a security token known as STO (something regarded as a new form of IPO) as opposed to ICO.

What is ICO?

"ICO is a process of issuing a public coin or token. It is similar to companies entering an initial public offering (IPO) by listing their stock (or shares) on a public stock exchange, such as the NYSE or NASDAQ. Coins or tokens are issued on blockchain, which means they are unregulated. They can be easily traded, but this is where it gets tricky." - Myk Pono

While companies in ICOs issue tokens, companies in IPO issue stocks. Tokens represents the utility in a particular project - it indicate in units what amount of utility a participant is entitled to when the project goes live while stocks represents right or ownership to the company.

ICO (Initial Coin Offering) since the inception of Bitcoin has become the top buzz word of the world of cryptocurrency and blockchain in general. It can also be understood as a means of raising funds through crowdfunding and private sales with cryptocurrencies (majorly BTC or ETH) to cater for and improve the infrastructure and token of a blockchain-based project. What has made ICO successful over the years couldn't be far from the belief that blockchain based projects are done with the interest of the public rather than to a central authority due to its inherent consensus algorithm - more so that the mother coin, bitcoin have this goal on top of every other features. ICO till now has also always been done in exchange for Bitcoin as the legal tender - so that humanly "trust" to a consensus rather than from an authority has always made the idea of ICO novel.

ICO funded project are mostly not always regulatory compliant leaving investors to speculation and or high level of risk in that there is no guarantee of a return of investment - since tokens sold during ICO doesn't fall in the category of a security offering. A reason that has made ICO projects prone to scams - making projects with enshrouded mission also scaling through and scamming people of their funds.

The first ICO was done in 2013 by a man named J. R. Willet aka founder of ICO. He proposed a new layer on top of the existing Bitcoin layer that would enable for innovation and other use case of Bitcoin infrastructure - from where he raised funds for his project known as Mastercoin (now called Omni). The idea as contained in his WhitePaper titled, "The Second Bitcoin Whitepaper", he listed some functions where he got the minds of people to believe and invest in the project without a security - birthing ICO. (To quote the summary: "We claim that the existing bitcoin network can be used as a protocol layer, on top of which new currency layers with new rules can be built …. We further claim that the new protocol layers … will provide initial funds to hire developers to build software which implements the new protocol layers, and … will richly reward early adopters of the new protocol.") Following this development in ICO, was Ethereum, which raised 3,700 BTC in 12 hours approximately USD $2.3 at the time. Since then, ICO has become a household name of blockchain and cryptocurrency especially in 2017 with first quarter of 2018 grossing over the total amount of ICO proceed in 2017 - is something that cannot be talked less about. Not until now when some people hiding under the cloud are beginning to hijack the system - causing fraud and making many countries to enact stringent laws against ICO funded organizations with many others being clamped upon. These among many reasons is raising a new form of seed funding for blockchain based projects known as ISO, which will be talked about later in this chapter.

How to invest in ICO

Investing in ICO is simple, just like investing in cryptocurrency (explained above). The only difference is that, in ICO, you are investing in a yet to exist coin. You're simply speculating with your legal tender to hope on the potential of a future coin through the token issued. You would need to following 3 process while investing in ICO.

i. Buy a legal tender (ETH or BTC) from an exchange. Since most ICO issuing project often use ERC20, then you're most likely to buy ETH. Since there are no place to buy cryptocurrency with fiat, you should use an exchange such as Coinbase.com.

ii. Setup a wallet: Setting up your wallet is simple, Blockchain's wallet tops my list. unlike MyEtherWallet, you can setup more than one wallet address with one app. Setting up your wallet would require getting and documenting your private key in the most secure way. Setting up your wallet is synonymous with signing up with a bank for an account number. The difference is that, with a bank, you do not have a private key leaving you with less control of your account. This is not so with a cryptocurrency wallet. With a cryptocurrency wallet, you have almost absolute control over your wallet - with the help of a private key. Once you receive coins into your wallet, it would be broadcasted throughout the network with masternodes, and miners (depending on the blockchain protocol) confirming that the coin was sent. To spend this coin in your wallet, you would need a private key to do so. Without it, your money cannot be spent or charged unlike the fiat system - leaving you with almost absolute control of your account.

iii. Research ICO: This is perhaps the hardest part in investing in ICO. It's the point you make decision regarding the project you will invest in. At this point, you will have to deploy your resources to activate your contract. To make this the best way, you would need a thorough search to evaluate some projects before deciding on which one to invest in. It would interest you to know that several ICO projects runs every day and simultaneously some days so getting to know your evaluation criteria is paramount choosing the best project. The following key points should help you in your search for the best ICO to invest in.

    a. Look at their product or prototype. A good ICO should have some level of traction, and if they are newly formed team, they should have some prototype of the solution their product is providing. A good insight into this will help you understand the value of the ICO's token, and this should be clear enough that it is understood.

    b. Team: Understanding who is behind a project helps to gauge the amount of trust or credibility that can be accrued to such a project. Knowing who the members of a team are can also suggest the market value such project. Think of it on what could make Ethereum raise 3,700 BTC in 12 hours. This is not to say if you don't see another Satoshi or Vitalik in a project you shouldn't invest. No! The idea is that members of a project team should be traceable (at least LinkedIn) for a start. A project packed full with team members with broken LinkedIn links or whose members' profile doesn't depict they are part of the team, should be avoided. You should also look at the team's contribution to blockchain on Github - this will help you understand the team's level of interest in the community.

Other things you should look at is their documents - like the whitepaper, token sale agreement, and more. Their token sale agreement will help you understand if the token is a security token or a utility token - all these will help you in making an informed decision. If you feel the project is exciting and you would want to dabble in more. Then, you may want to join their community so you could get periodic update as well as also evaluate the project in real-time.

Also always have it as the back of your mind that there is no guarantee of getting a good or even any return on your investment. So you should invest as much as you can lose, and if it turns out good, you earn massively. It's an extremely risky investment as there is currently no regulation against ICO except those that falls in as a security token (and if this is the case, then it won't be an ICO).

How to Promote ICO

It's almost impossible to have an ICO project with organic community interest except for existing projects with solid traction prior ICO (Telegram is an example of a project with traction hence organic cryptocurrency community interest) yet promotion was never substituted for anything. If you're running an ICO project one of the major challenges you will face is getting investors to see your project and buy into your idea. This is even becoming hard as there are many other projects shrouding the community on daily basis. The distortion in crypto communities are much and this is where a good project is separated from a bad one (your tenacity in pushing your idea to the community it what counts especially if it's novel).

1). Your Website. In promoting ICO, your website should be the center for all the traffic - every SEO and PPC put together should have your website at the centre while making consideration. Your website copy should tell it all. Including videos, decks - that put together gives a layman and in depth overview of what your project is all about. In promoting your ICO with your website as the stop shop, you should consider the including the followings:

- A short explainer videos
- Your white paper
- Project team
- Roadmap.

They are essential items you shouldn't play with when designing your website as your marketing tool. Other things that are required to make your website meet your goal are a clear CTA (call-to-action). Depending on the stage of your ICO, you may want to invite them to test your prototype, join your Telegram community, and many others. Each of your objective should be met with a clear CTA.

2). PR and Media Outreach. Press release and media outreaches are great ways to spread the news about your ICO project. Using professional PR companies would yield great results however there are DIY approach such that also help if you have a tight budget. Some of the DIY approach include:

- Guest blog posts on cryptocurrency blogs with backlinks to your website.
- Using Crypto YouTube influencers with clear CTA.
- Participating in meetups such as Blockshow and many others to communicate your ICO in person.

3). Social Media Marketing (SMM), and Community Management. Social media cannot be done without. Social media networks such as Reddit, Facbook, Quora, LinkedIn, Twitter, and Telegram all put together would give you a perfect knack on your SMM strategy.

These social media platforms function uniquely and should be followed adequately to avoid been viewed as a hyped project. Quora for example, you could write quality article to contribute in the ICO thread with backlink to your website. For Reddit, you could comment, contribute to threads same as LinkedIn, and can use Twitter for broadcasts. Other ways to promote your ICO are using bounty programs, airdrops, and PPC ads.

ICO yesterday and ICO today

Cryptocurrency cycle cannot be said to have exceeded its infancy stage as it's yet a decade old. However, there has been some significant changes in one of the most popular activity in cryptocurrency projects, and it's about the recent issue surrounding ICO.

With recent regulations and subsequent clamp down on deceptive projects identified as scams, many organizations and projects who intend to crowdfund are rethinking and while others such as Telegram withdrew their ICO from the public, some are totally changing and instead bowing to the long-awaited pressure from Venture Capitalists (VCs). VCs such as Wall Street are private investors in public equity, and this means for companies to issue a security to investors, there must be accurate level of compliant with SEC and other relating regulations before they can put up their stocks for buy in a way of IPO but with cryptocurrency – in the form of Security Token Offering (STO).

ICO has metamorphosed from what is use to be – a utility token offering to a security token offering. While many feel this development will stall the rate of scam associated with the cryptocurrency industry, some others feel, it's a step to deter the spread of the Bitcoin's dream of decentralized digital currency. Pro ICO believes is that first, relegating ICO to STO will stall innovation and suppress the masses' willingness to invest in projects they feel is for the community interest – making VCs to invest in project will replicate the same thing done in fiat in cryptocurrency. While pro STO believes that mitigating the risk associated with cryptocurrency is what will make the world a better place. But the truth is STO is far behind the goal of Bitcoin, which arguably cause the spread and interest in cryptographic digital currency.

Chapter 4

Understanding blockchain and its application

This Chapter

In this chapter, we will take a look at what blockchain technology is, its history and how it differs from decentralized ledger technology (DLT)

BLOCKCHAIN

What Is Blockchain?

The Wikipedia encyclopedia defines blockchain as a growing list of records called blocks which are linked using cryptography. The lists of records are called blocks, and each of new blocks contain a cryptographic hash of the previous block; a timestamp and transaction data. Blockchain is designed to be immutable - meaning, block records cannot be changed and reversed: solving the problem of double spending. Making it an open distributed ledger that has the capacity to efficiently record transactions between two parties, and do so in a verifiable and immutable way.

Because it is widely used as a distributed ledger, the management of a blockchain application is done by a peer-to-peer network which accurately conforms to a protocol for internode communication and the validation of new blocks. Once the block has been recorded, the data for any of them cannot be modified or altered retroactively without undergoing an alteration of all the subsequent blocks, which demands a consensus of the majority of the network. Despite the fact that blockchain records are not unalterable, blockchain is widely considered very secure by design, as it exemplifies a distributed computing system with high Byzantine fault tolerance. Owing to this, the blockchain has subsequently been claimed with have a decentralized consensus.

According to Don and Alex Tapscott, the authors of a book titled Blockchain Revolution (2016), the blockchain is an incorruptible digital ledger of economic transactions that can be programmed to record not just financial transactions but virtually everything of value. The author of Technology Futurist, Ian Khan, the blockchain, as revolutionary much as it sounds as a revolution, is truly a mechanism to bring all and sundry to the echelon of accountability. According to him, blockchain brings with it the promises/reality of no more missed transactions, human or machine errors, or even an exchange that was not executed with the consent of the parties involved. In his words, "Above everything else, the most critical areas where blockchain helps is to guarantee the validity of a transaction by recording it not only on a main register, but on a connected system of registers, all of which are connected via a secure validation mechanism".

The inventor of Ethereum, Vitalik Buterin, says that blockchain is the ultimate solution to the problem of manipulation, saying that the technology's opportunities are the "highest in the countries that haven't reached that level yet". Information that is store on a blockchain exists as a shared and continually reconciled database – a way of using the network that has obvious benefits. Being that the database of this technology isn't stored in a single location; the records kept therein are truly public and easily verifiable.

How It Came About?

Being that blockchain came into advent along with cryptocurrency, the technology was invented by Satoshi Nakamoto in 2008 to serve as a ledger for public transaction for Bitcoin – the very first digital currency. This invention made Bitcoin the first cryptocurrency to solve the double-spending problem without seeking permission for a trusted, central authority or server. Its design served as an inspiration for other applications, and the blockchain which is readable by the public is widely utilized by the lot of cryptocurrencies.

What was recorded as the first work on a cryptographically secured chain of blocks dates as far back as 1991 – a process engaged by the duo of Stuart Haber and W. Scott Stornetta. These two looked to implement a system where the timestamps of systems could not be backdated or tampered with. In 1992, Bayer, Haber, and Stornetta incorporated Merkle trees to the design – a move which greatly enhanced its efficiency by allowing several documents to be collected into one block.

The first 'blockchain' concept was then brought first by a person or group of persons who prefer to go by the pseudonym Satoshi Nakamoto and it was implemented in 1009 as a core component of the cryptocurrency Bitcoin. Then in August 2014, the

Bitcoin blockchain file, which comprised the records of all the transactions that have occurred on the network, leveled up to 20 GB. In January of 2015, the size of the block has undergone an increment in size to nearly 30 GB. From January 2016 through to 2017, the Bitcoin blockchain size went from 50 GB to 100 GB.

It is important to note here that the phrases 'block' and 'chain' were used separately in the original paper which Satoshi Nakamoto made public. As time went on, they were eventually popularized as the single word 'blockchain' by 2016. The term Blockchain 2.0 refers to new applications of the distributed blockchain database, making its first emergence in 2014. This second generation of programmable blockchain, along with its implementation, was described by The Economist as one that comes with a "programmable language that allows users to write more sophisticated smear contracts, thus bringing about invoices that pay themselves when a shipment arrives or share certificates which automatically send their owners dividends if profits reach a specific level".

Through the data storage process across it unique kind of network, blockchain technology eliminates the risks that come with data being held as the center. Its network is in the lacking of centralized points of vulnerability which computer hackers can easily exploit – which means it's safe. The internet which people use today is filled with security problems in the many, which everyone is quite familiar with. Contrasting

to our conventional reliance on usernames and passwords to access social media accounts privately and protect our identity as well as assets, the upgrade which is blockchain has methods that make use of encryption technology. This basis upon which this is built are called the public and private keys. A public key, which is a long randomly generated string of numbers, is the users' address on the blockchain. Cryptocurrencies sent across the network get recorded as components affiliated to that address. The private key is a password-like element that gives its owner access to his/her cryptocurrency as well as other digital assets. Anyone that stores data on the blockchain network is said to be guaranteeing information that is incorruptible.

In accordance to Accenture, an application of the diffusion of innovations theory suggests that the blockchain technology and network attained a 13.5 percent rate of adoption with financial services in 2016, reaching the early adopters stage.

Blockchain and DLT

There is a common misconception aimed at taking advantage of the cryptocurrency buzz, and it's with conventional companies, banks and government-owned institutions coming out to say they're adopting the use of blockchain technology in their operation. The Bank of England for example, said they were taking a look into the use of blockchain and Distributed Ledger Technology (DLT) to make a Real Time Gross Settlement efficient as much as possible). In many case this is done to gain massive support from the cryptocurrency community as the mere usage of "blockchain" in a project is synonymous with community support. However, it's clear to differentiate this word especially in a book like this as it would help investors properly determine which project will deliver the community and consensus goal of blockchain technology - so you don't invest in another stock in the guise of tokens.

Distributed Ledger Technology

DLT is a database of records used to store and confirm records in real time across several data point. Transactions on a DLT networks are recorded in multiple places at the same time. DLT has been a popular knowledge for millennials in paper form but only became operational in the advent and spread of computers in the late 20th century. At the time till now, banks used it the most - especially as seen during the transition from NEFT (National Electronic Fund Transfer) to RTGS (Real Time Gross Settlement) which enabled the processing and broadcasting of transactions across concerned banking institutions anywhere in the world in real time, is a function of DLT but with a central authority designing the structure of each data point. Each data point or nodes in a banking DLT could serve as each banking institution in each country with bigger nodes serving as their central banks who determines the communication structure of its data points with other data points. In other words, a central authority will still needed to confirm that the transaction was processed with best practice. For example, banks confirms financial transactions and central bank audits the banks for each transaction to be sure transactions are performed with best practice depending on each country's foreign policy on banking (and this is almost the cut for blockchain technology).

BLOCKCHAIN

Everything about DLT is about blockchain as blockchain is a form of DLT or you can see DLT as the basic form of blockchain technology. In practice, to run a blockchain technology, you may first want to run it on a private network like a DLT to have a feel before deploying it to the blockchain networks. One thing to take home is that, with blockchain, transactions settled within the network is final, near-ubiquitous, and immutable. With the use of cryptography, it's impossible for a third party to oversee the transactions on a blockchain network as possible on DLT network. With blockchain, transactions are cryptographically signed and broadcasted throughout the network with the longest chain in the block winning the validation and creating a new block with the preceding chain impossible to edit. Due to the successful implementation of blockchain and its cryptography, it's become one of the most popular application of blockchain apparently always used interchangeably and sometimes with the intention to get support. They are not synonymous!

Going Forward

International Business Machine launched a blockchain innovation research center in Singapore in July 2016. In November the same year, a working group of people for the World Economic Forum had a meet to discuss the development of governance models related to the blockchain. And in May 2018, Gartner discovered that only 1 percent of CIOs indicated any kind of blockchain adoption within their organization. He also found that only 8 percent of the CIOs were in the short-term 'planning or active experimentation with blockchain.

BLOCKCHAIN TECHNOLOGY USE CASES

As has been earlier established, blockchain technology serves up something of a game-changer in for our current record systems and infrastructure. It could be thought of as a permanent, immutable, decentralized, and trustless ledger that can be used for the storage of all manner of records.

Having become the subject of interest from a great many individuals and institutions since formally coming into existence, the technology is beginning to see increased use cases for entrepreneurs in various around the globe who are looking to leverage the benefits of this nascent technology in the area of bringing about development and solutions to problems in their respective fields.

Blockchain technology holds a lot of potential and with the breakthroughs recorded in recent times, imaginations are running wild. The design of the technology makes it suitable for use in any area in that has need for trustworthy and unalterable records. Blockchain technology also places absolute cryptography power in the hands of individuals, eliminating any need for centralized transaction authorities for what are generally referred to as 'pull transactions'.

Of course, there is a lot of buzz surrounding the potential impact of the technology and even though some of the hype is yet to be justified, it takes nothing away from the notion that the technology can come in handy in a lot of scenarios. And the fact that it is not that hard to dream up high-level use cases for the application of the technology also does prove a point.

Some of the world's brightest minds when it comes to innovation and technology have left no one in doubt as per the myriad of ways the technology can be applied to some of the lingering problems bedeviling today's world. Whether the technology is suitable for a particular scenario is a function of the specifics and the needs of that scenario, but in any case, there are a number of cases in which using the technology does seem like a perfect solution. Now, here are ways in which blockchain technology can be put to use.

KEEPING RECORDS:

Digital Identity. The provision of an opportunity to create a strong system of digital identity is, perhaps, one of the strongest points of blockchain technology. Since individuals are afforded control and ownership of cryptographic keys, it does bring about new possibilities for the creation of digital relationships.

The technology affords its users a new and secure way to manage identity in the digital world by eliminating any need to divulge too much personal information that could cause some sort of vulnerability. And this quality is down to a combination of factors which include the fact that;

- Blockchain technology is not based on accounts and permissions associated with accounts.

- The technology is based on push transactions.

- Ownership of private keys implies ownership of the digital asset.

Tokenization

Blockchain technology also proves useful in the area of tokenization, which generally involves the authentication of a unique physical item with a corresponding digital asset that is in the form of a token. Such details as intellectual property, fraud detection, supply-chain management, inter-organizational data management, as well as anti-counterfeiting, can be handled effectively and efficiently by exploring the digital token function of the technology; a feature that will come in handy for numerous institutions whose services cut across the aforementioned fields. The technology means a lot more than maintaining a database, it is built with a view to managing vital systems of record as it represents a veritable solution to the challenges associated with information gathering and data collection.

For Government Records. Some of the record-keeping qualities of blockchain technology can also be also be exploited by organized governments in various parts of the world. As a matter of fact, there are three key areas in which the technology can prove helpful.

The first one revolves around ownership rights which govern the possession, revocation, generation, replacement, or loss of cryptographic keys. The second area that piques the interest of the government is the subject of who can play a part in a blockchain network. And last but not least, governments have an interest in blockchain protocols that have the capacity to authorize transactions.

This can come in handy in attempts to regulate the stock market or authorize the format of market exchange trades. It is for this singular reason that many blockchain developers regard its application in regulatory compliance as an ample business opportunity.

For Trailing Audits in Financial Institutions. Banks and other large financial institutions that are at the center of helping individuals form digital relationships over the web can secure holders' account information by exploiting the server-client infrastructure.

While banks are suited to the idea of spending billions for the purpose of keeping transaction data secure, businesses remain susceptible to hack attacks which can sometimes result in the leaking of sensitive financial information.

With a view to mitigating that lingering bottleneck, blockchain technology can be leveraged as it provides a means of automatically creating records of who has been privy to what information or records, as well as well who have accessed it. The technology also allows for setting up controls as a way of granting or denying access to classified information to specific individuals with specific designations. Health records of the government is another area where the technologies reach can also be put to use.

AS A PLATFORM:

For Smart Contracting. Blockchain technology makes for the the formation and security of strong and binding digital relationships. Through the incorporation of smart contracts, the technology can be used to process information and documents stored in blockchains for the purpose of supporting complex legal agreements.

This can come in handy when agreements need to be set in stone between banks, insurance companies, startups, and a number of other institutions. Smart contracts written on the blockchain can also form the operational models of many businesses.

Smart contracts are a product of blockchain technology. They are a combination of Ricardian contracts and coded business logic. They are triggered only by the fulfillment of specific requirements which are commands encoded on the blockchain. If these requirements are not met, they are programmed to not take effect. Agreements written on smart contracts can be altered or changed; an actual case of something being "set in stone".

There is also another development in the form of institutions who work on offshoots of the blockchain, which are like customized or bespoke blockchains created on the backs of the larger public blockchains. Problems and debates associated with the 'block size', as is prevalent with Bitcoin, are being sidestepped through the adoption of such arrangements. In many quarters, establishments of this nature are also being tipped to create blockchains that have the capacity to authorize pretty specific types of transactions.

Ethereum actually appears to have taken the blockchain platform idea a step further as it seeks to apply business logic on a blockchain with a view to supporting the coding of transactions of any degree of complexity, which is then followed by the grant or denial of authorization by the network that controls the code.

As put forward by its creator, Vitalik Buterin, the purpose of the Ethereum blockchain adaptation is to enable the coding of smart contracts. The coding process typically involves the exploration of programs that control blockchain assets, and the subsequent execution by a blockchain protocol that is running on the Ethereum network in this case.

For Automated Governance. Bitcoin and other similar projects, when looked at from a different perspective, can be extrapolated to somewhat indicate an experiment in governance because these items themselves are examples of automated governance; something also referred to as Decentralized Autonomous Organization (DAO). While there may still be a dearth in literature on the subject, the Bitcoin and other similar systems appear to be serving up subtle lessons in how blockchain technology can be leveraged in the future of governance.

For Markets. Here is another way of looking at cryptocurrency: Think of it as a digital bearer bond. What this basically implies is that it can also serve as a means of creating an identity that is digitally-unique to enable the control of code that have particular ownership rights with keys. These tokens can be deduced to represent the idea that ownership of code can stand in for a stock, or any other physical item/asset. Transaction rules for these instruments can be coded as specific instructions by a blockchain protocol.

For Streamlining Of Clearing and Settlement. The term 'T + 3' is quite common in the world of stock trading... In those quarters, this has a meaning that construed to imply that three (3) days have to pass before a trade (T) is accepted or settled. Fair enough, there are other ways through this time lag can be significantly reduced but none of them promise security and/or absence of risk. And this is where blockchain technology really does distinguish itself as trade is basically settlement with adoption of the technology in trading; implying zero downtime. This, amongst others, are ways in which blockchain technology can revolutionize the world of finance.

For Automating Regulatory Compliance. Blockchain technology does a lot more than just serve as a storehouse for information. It can also do a good job of enhancing and enabling regulatory compliance through the use of code. Essentially, what this means is that the manner in which blocks are granted validity can serve as the basis for the translation of government legal prose into digital content.

For banks, this could also mean fostering efficacy and efficiency in anti-money laundering (AML) compliance. Blockchain technology can be customized to perform different functions, including the permission of transactions, as well as the flagging of certain transactions based on a set of rules that define the grounds for signalling the existence of an unscrupulous or shady transaction. Banks are thus afforded a veritable medium for automatic regulatory reporting, as well as automatic authorization of transactions.

Chapter 5

The Story of Bitcoin and Altcoins

This Chapter

Writing a book about cryptocurrency without going down the lane of Bitcoin and Altcoin wouldn't be complete, and this chapter is dedicated to bringing you some memorable history of Bitcoin and the emergence of Altcoin.

What Does Cryptocurrency have to do With Blockchain Anyway?

There goes a common misconception about cryptocurrencies and blockchain technology that recognizes the blockchain as a revolutionary way of sharing information, a clearly valuable and transformative technology – but cryptocurrencies are just a fad, the latest buzz from the tech world. So why all the fuss about cryptocurrencies, anyway? These two elements are intricately entwined. In fact, they are inseparable.

Make no mistake about it; the tokens that make up cryptocurrencies – from Bitcoin, to Ether, to Monero – are the mediums through which one participates in public blockchain protocols. This is not optional. It is a fundamental feature of the technology. If a public blockchain protocol is valuable, then the tokens through which one participates in it accrue value, although there is a slight deviation from this if the blockchain in question is a private blockchain (which we shall look at soon enough).

Technically, "cryptocurrency" is a misnomer. You'll hardly find one that functions like regular currency. Investments in cryptocurrencies should not be considered foreign exchange trading. It helps to regard cryptocurrencies as digital assets associated with the value of a particular blockchain protocol. A common reason for this misconception is that Bitcoin was initially billed as a currency. But since its inception, a variety of digital assets has emerged and even Bitcoin itself is now best regarded as a store of value rather than the traditional currency for which it was initially pegged. And there are currently many of them in existence, many of them less than worthwhile, poorly-engineered fads. We shall walk through the nitty-gritty of some of them as this work progresses but first let's walk through to memory lane.

Brief History of Cryptocurrencies and Blockchain Networks

"Bitcoin: A Peer-to-Peer Electronic Cash System". So read the title of the Satoshi Nakamoto's (a pseudonym) revolutionary paper which marked the birth of the Bitcoin into the internet in November, 2008. In its own words, the paper described "a system for electronic transactions without relying on trust". The 2009 launch of bitcoin was the first real life application of blockchain technology, though the idea had long been conceived. For the five years that followed, the history of blockchain would remain nearly synonymous with the history of Bitcoin.

2014 would mark yet another milestone in blockchain's illustrious history. The application of blockchain technology had hitherto been limited to cryptocurrency. Although the Bitcoin protocol had proven itself in that realm, there was a dearth of scripting language required to develop blockchain applications with functionality beyond simply serving as a cryptocurrency.

In stepped Vitalik Buterin, a prominent Bitcoin enthusiast for several years who had already co-founded Bitcoin Magazine in 2012, at the precocious age of 18, to remedy the situation. Buterin and his team of programmers developed a brand new blockchain protocol featuring the so-called "smart contracts" that made it possible for programmers to build scripts into his blockchain that act as contractual agreements and execute automatically when certain conditions are met. Ethereum; that's what he called this new blockchain. Since inception in 2014, the Ethereum blockchain has witnessed significant growth and is now in the running with Bitcoin in the crème de la crème of blockchains. Many other cryptocurrencies have since popped up on the backs of this technology. To this very day, Satoshi Nakamoto remains a myth as no one has an idea who he is/was. What is public knowledge, however, is that the first open source Bitcoin client was released in January 2009 and over the next few years, Satoshi Nakamoto amassed around 1 million Bitcoins before going under the radar around mid-2010. This vast Bitcoin bounty remains untouched to this day and is spread across a myriad of Bitcoin accounts.

Bitcoin and Altcoins

Digital currency is no doubt starting to take over the financial and economic mainstay of the world. Hard currency is fast going out of the stream, as different types of online coins emerge for safer and more profiting business transactions. The most popular of these digital currencies is the Bitcoin. Even if most people are not very conversant with how it works, at least they have some levels of familiarity with it, and understand that it is majorly an investment initiative. Generally, these digital currencies are known as cryptocurrencies, and altcoins are an intriguing part of them. The word "altcoin" is an abbreviated representation of "alternative Bitcoin" or Bitcoin alternative". This means that altcoin is a descriptive word for all other forms of cryptocurrency other than Bitcoin. It is so because at some point, most altcoins are designed to either act as replacement or improvement of at least one distinctive component of a Bitcoin. Examples are Zcash, triple, Monero, dash, Litecoin, Dogecoin, Nxt, BitShares, etc. According to the researches and publications of CoinMarketCap online organization, there are over 478 altcoins in the digital marketplaces. Nevertheless, more continue to appear each day, such as the Darkcoin.

Having had a foundational establishment that altcoins are closely associated with bitcoins, it also of necessity to mention that most, if not all of these coins, are little more than Bitcoin clones, which change some minor characteristics such as transaction speed, distribution method or hashing algorithm. Most of these coins usually have short lifespans, except for Litecoin, which was one of the first altcoins, and using a different hashing algorithm than Bitcoin, has had higher number of currency units, and is now referred to as "Bitcoin gold".

Altcoins have differentiating features from Bitcoin in various ways; some having different economic modeling, or a different coin-distribution method, as in altcoins that were given away to all legal citizens of a country. Some altcoins are advanced and beneficial, while some are not. The former perform useful special tasks for users while others do not really have any usefulness.

The main aim of Bitcoin is to attain a decentralized financial system. And, altcoins are developed to further the decentralization, although most enthusiast and practitioners opine and argue that they are not necessary due to the fact that they cannot compete with the technical makeup and uniqueness of Bitcoin. The cryptocurrency community has however been helped by altcoins, as they allow developer to experiment with a wide range of uniquely developed features. Also, altcoins give Bitcoin a healthy competition, giving the users of cryptocurrencies various alternative options, thereby, forcing the developers of Bitcoin to strive to remain active and keep up coming up with peculiar innovations. In a way, this makes Bitcoin and altcoins equally and similarly useful.

Various Types of Cryptocurrencies and How They Work

As earlier stated, cryptocurrencies are those mediums through which one gets to participate in blockchain protocols. They are digital or virtual assets designed to work as a medium of exchange. They use cryptography to secure and verify transactions, as well as to control the creation of new units of a particular cryptocurrency. There are hundreds of them currently in existence but we shall narrow our explanation down to the most popular ones that have gained some form of traction.

Bitcoin

This was the first of what has come to be known as "cryptocurrencies". They are forms of digital money that use encryption to secure transactions and keep the creation of new units in check. The creation of this cryptocurrency was inspired by the quest for a currency that is outside the jurisdiction or control of governments or institutions that you could trade globally and anonymously with no restrictions. Bitcoin is regarded as the mother of all other

cryptocurrencies, as all other cryptocurrencies are more or less copycats, and are collectively referred to as alternate bitcoin (altcoin). They were the creation of the anonymous developer who goes by the pseudonym, Satoshi Nakamoto in 2008, and have since exploded onto the global financial scene. The cryptocurrency uses cryptographic proof instead of trust, allowing any two willing parties to transact directly with each other without the need for a trusted third party. This kind of stateless, bank-free currency utilizes a distributed, cryptographically-secure blockchain to record payment transactions. Payments recorded onto the blockchain are powered by the users, who offer their computer power. What lies in the offing as rewards are newly-created Bitcoin, and this activity is referred to as mining. Their value, just like most things, is determined by demand and supply. Bitcoin has hit the mainstream over the last few months as the decentralized digital currency continuous to hit outrageous heights.

Altcoins

Ethereum: Ethereum is a fast growing and rapidly evolving digital currency. It is also an altcoin or alternate coin because its roots are from the well-known Bitcoin. Ethereum is a form of decentralized cryptocurrency that with the blockchain and mathematical algorithms embedded in the development, can run extensive and well defined smart contracts across international borders. The ethereum digital currency smart contract comprises applications that can functions and deliver exactly as they have been programmed, without any sudden chances of downtime, overseeing or censorship, fraud or any intrusions from online and offline third parties. Litecoin is a very open-sourced, enterprise and blockchain-developed platform with smart contract functions that aide users to monitor and oversee their own financial transactions.

While Bitcoins aims to disrupt the essence of PayPal and its likes, as well as online banking, ethereum is aimed with blockchain technology, to replace all forms and calibers of internet third parties, especially those that usually store irrelevant data, transfer mortgages and keep records of financial tools.

In semblance to the altcoin litecoin and other digital currencies, the ethereum cryptocurrency has a wallet system called Ethereum Wallet which acts as a portal through which users can access a decentralized application software on the Ethereum blockchain. The Ethereum Wallet enables each user to have a firm holding and security ether and other assets related that are built too with Ethereum components. These internet protocols allows users to write, deploy, manage and use smart contracts.

Litecoin: Litecoin digital currency is a peer-to-peer digital currency or cryptocurrency, and an open software project launched beneath the affiliation of the MIT/X11 internet license, which gives the user the upper hand, with which he will run, modify and copy the entailments of the software, and to disperse at his options as well, modified copies of the same software. The software with which the Litecoin is developed and ran is released in a see-through procedure that with blockchain, gives all the needed room for independent confirmation of binaries as well as all of their corresponding source codes.

Litecoin, an altcoin, or alternate coin, is overseen by a mathematical system that keeps it secure, empowering individuals to have reasonable and total control over their financial activities. Litecoin, with the help of the blockchain technology that is used to develop it, has features that offer fast time tracking confirmation on financial transactions, and has a very efficient storage system for the safekeeping of financial history details. Due to its help in the economic and financial industry, having considered the volume of trade and liquidity, Litecoin has been confirmed to be a commercial medium closely complementary to Bitcoin. The Litecoin blockchain has the ability of handling and reflecting protocols of higher capacities than its counterpart, Bitcoin. This digital currency supports more financial operations, having no need to cast modifications on the software in the future, because it is embedded with a more frequent generation of blockchain. Litecoin is also developed with a very definite, secure and basic wallet encryption. This allows a user to with entered passwords access his account to view transactions, and account balances. The same secure wallet encryption system wards off viruses and unidentified Trojans that invade, corrupt and steal from wallets, and it always enables the user to run sanity checks before making payments.

Monero: Also abbreviated to be known as XMR, is an open source digital currency which was developed to provide users with the decentralized merchant system and overall scalability, and that can be run on Windows, Mac, Linux, FreeBSD and Android Operating Systems.

The Monero digital coin or alternative currency was launched in April 2014 as a medium through which credible online financial privacy can be accessed and maintained, at all costs. At the point of official announcement, it was made available for users from international borders to access and use for making payments, garnering profits and managing funds.

Monero is decentralized cryptocurrency, which means that it will be of extreme difficulty for internet fraudsters and Trojans to hack into and access the accounts of the users to monitor their financial transactions and steal their funds. All transactions related to Monero altcoin are always confirmed by a distributed consensus, and then recorded on the blockchain technology used to develop and secure it. There are no third parties or intermediaries on the Monero platform. It gains all the available benefits of a decentralized digital currency, without any of the standard privacy concessions, interfaces or popups. All addresses and details of transactions are untraceable as with the Monero blockchain, profiles cannot be linked to any particular user or real-world identity.

Dash: Dash coin is a digital currency; an altcoin that was built, developed and launched to enhance at least one of the components of Bitcoin. Bitcoin is also a digital currency that is just as known and just as developed, having many features that it cannot carry alone, hence the emergence of altcoins, also called alternative coins, like the dash. Dash is a portmanteau of digital cash.

Dash, also known as dark coin and Xcoin, is a cryptocurrency in the economic digital system that has an open sourced user-to-user nature that offers to customers all the same features as its affiliating predecessor, the Bitcoin. The only difference between the dash coin and Bitcoin is that its features are developed with faster capabilities with prompt time signatures as it manifests in instant transactions, private transactions and a decentralized government system. It is as a result of Dash's unique decentralized governance and budgeting system platform that made it to be recognized as the first (but not necessarily the foremost) decentralized independent online financial transaction system.

Ripple. This is more or less like a gateway or portal through which payments can be made to and from international borders. Ideally, it is a payment protocol that is real time, reliable and provable. Ripple is a colossal settlement system, currency exchange platform and remittance network developed by the Ripple Company. As such, it is as well called the Ripple Transaction Protocol (RTXP) or ripple protocol. It is built and developed on an open source internet mechanism, consensus ledger and native currency called XRP (ripples).

Ripple is a distributed ledger system that has been adopted by banks and payment networks as settlement infrastructure, because from the financial institutions" perspectives, the ripple system has quite a number of merits that makes it surpass all other existing cryptocurrencies like Bitcoin, and alternate coins like litecoin, dogecoin, Zcash, etc. It is adopted also due to its very catchy price and promising security network.

On larger yet more concise terms, the Ripple payment protocol connects banks, payment providers and corporate organizations through the Ripple network in order to offer services, entailing seamless experiences that enable all and sundry to send and receive money globally. It is built on one of the most advanced blockchain technologies that to large extents, are scalable, totally secure, and interoperates a vast majority of networks. It provides also, the optional access to the world's fastest and most scalable digital asset for international financial transactions.

Zcash: Zcash is a digital currency that was said to have been sprouted from the Zerocion project, which was armed to with some features improving anonymity for all the users of Bitcoin. The Zerocoin financial internet protocol upon initial improvement and transformation, yielded the Zcash cryptocurrency in 2016.

One very important and great attribute of the Zcash digital currency is that is allows private investors to have the options of conducting a selective disclosure, which then affords them the avenue to have proof of their payments for auditing purposes. Also, Zcash affords all the private investors on the platform the choice of complying with all the available online bodies that help fight against money laundering or excessive tax regulations.

With the Zcash cryptocurrency and its backup blockchain technology, transactions for users are very auditable, but the entire disclosure of the details in under the total control of the participant, not the middle men or any overseeing body means that the Zcash through this medium promotes decentralization, making it available to all users in order have a completely private financial activity that is not being monitored by an online banking system or any other intermediary of the sort.

The payment made with Zcash bitcoin cryptocurrency are broadcast on a general blockchain, which is public, but the users of the digital currency have access to a non-mandatory privacy feature that helps the sender, receiver and amount that is being transacted on a regular and guaranteed basis.

Cryptocurrency Success Stories

It does not make complete sense if we go on and on about what Bitcoin and other cryptocurrencies have to offer if we don't take out some time to really justify that these digital monies have helped people achieve a lot – with zero to hero stories in the many. There are many people out there who have had their own slices of the giant crypto cake, and are more than willing to share their stories with the rest of the world. While some countries are banning the currency majorly out of fear and uncertainty, people are looking upon it as a sham because of lack of information. These success stories go in many ways to prove that despite the many controversies hovering around this development, people are yet making a fortune out of the so called digital coins. While breakthroughs are relative, there are still lots of opportunities for ones who buy and/or sell Bitcoin, Ethereum, Dash, Ripple and many more. And if these people didn't emerge to the public front to testify how cryptocurrencies have turned their lives for the better, then it would be easier writing it off altogether. In no particular order, let's have some glimpses at these financial narratives.

The Winklevoss Brothers

Brothers Cameron and Tyler Winklevoss are perhaps a duo that can be said to be the most famous and crypto-rich people in the world. With a digital currency net worth of $10 billion, the twin siblings distinguish themselves from the crowd. These brothers were not initially cryptocurrency investors, as their names first became popular when they met out an accusation to Mark Zuckerberg for plagiarizing the ideas of the social network for Facbook. They even went as far as suing him to court. They did win the case against the tech giant, who paid them a settlement agreement of $65 million, though the twins were themselves accused of patent trolling.

It was with the amount paid to them that they made a foray down the path of cryptocurrency, spending around $11 million from the money to purchase Bitcoins. For the fact that the first digital currency was somewhat a cheap commodity then, the brothers bought lots of them. Half a decade later, their investments yielded fruits and made them become the first publicly known crypto-billionaires in the world. Cameron and Tyler's investment in Bitcoin is up more than 31,000%, and no one in the public has managed to repeat their kind of success.

Tim Draper

Tim Draper, who is today worth $270 million, is a popular venture investor and founder of Draper Fisher Jurveston. In spite of the reality that Tim's capital in crypto is obviously less than a billion, he yet makes the list as one of the most successful crypto investors. With $27 million only in Bitcoins, he worthy of contention, coupled with the fact that we are yet oblivious of the many other cryptocurrencies he has managed to invest in over the years.

In 2014, Tim Draper bought at an auction of the U.S marshals about 30, 000 Bitcoins from the number of crypto that was withdrawn from the wallets of the semi-criminal platform Silk Road. The businessman is yet optimistic about what the future holds as it regards digital currencies. Not long ago, he disclosed that the currencies' emergence is of more importance than the creation of the internet and the industrial revolution. Tim also forecast a growth of Bitcoin to $50,000 by the end of 2018. Whether or not this prediction comes true yet remains unclear, but what we are sure of is that Draper isn't going to hang his crypto boots anytime soon.

Roger Ver

With the nickname "Bitcoin Jesus" Roger is one of the first largest investors who starting doing business in the crypto market. It was during his stormy activities in the industry that he earned his reputation as well as his nickname. Various estimates posit that the entrepreneur owned about 300,000 Bitcoins, and today Roger is an active promoter of another digital currency called Bitcoin cash. According to his statements, he had all his Bitcoins sold out to begin his drive down the Bitcoin Cash Avenue.

Roger Ver is $27 million rich in crypto and the stakes just keep getting higher. His fortune has been analyzed on the backs of the fact that the millionaire still keeps Bitcoins with him or has bought Bitcoin Cash worth the same amount.

Kristofer Koch

Kristofer Koch is a Norwegian electrical engineer who decided to take his chances and invest 150 kroners in 5,000 Bitcoins in 2014. It was at the time that Bitcoin just started, with the idea being fairly new to people – many of them to say the least. Koch got introduced to cryptocurrency when he was writing a thesis on it. His investment was relatively meager, and that was why he forgot about it. He had no idea what the token can be worth until he came across a media coverage related to crypto success. Kristofer spent a long time trying to recover his private key in order to gain access to his wallet. When his efforts came through, he found one and discovered that he had 5,000 Bitcoins in his wallet, which converted to 5 million kroners or $886 million. Only 1,000 of the currency were enough cash to buy an apartment in the wealthy neighborhood of Toyen in Oslo. He had never imagined how well the $26.60 initial investment would pay off in the long run. With a house in his name and 4,000 Bitcoins still left in his wallet, this story is one of the many that would make us want to time-travel to the early Bitcoin days and invest perhaps all our fortunes.

Olaf-Carlson Wee

When Olaf-Carlson was 26 years old, in February of 2013, he was employed by a Bitcoin startup company. Bitcoin's value was at $20 to $30 at the time and people were still very new to the whole crypto concept – a factor that made him decide to get his monthly salary in Bitcoins. He saw the most spectacular rise in the cryptocurrency space and decided to go all in with his compensation at Coinbase. What tickled his speculative fancy was the idea of a decentralized means of payment behind Bitcoin. As of now, his money has exponentially grown due to the unchained success that comes with the token. While more and more people are starting to show interest in crypto, Wee is regarded as one of the first few persons who took the bull by the horn despite the odds.

Carlson's earliest investment in Bitcoin went down the drain when the currency crashed from $16 each to $2, but he yet believed in the system. He sent his resume to crypto wallet Coinbase and became the organizations first and foremost staff, where he gained commendable insights in the cryptocurrency with his many stints. By the Bitcoin started to soar high, Olaf had enough coins to make him a millionaire, after which he went on to found Polychain Capital, a blockchain asset hedge fund in 2017. This enterprise's assets swelled from $4 million to over $200 million in a matter of few months.

Jered Kenna

Jered Kenna can be regarded as one of the people who made a foray down the path of cryptocurrency and made it through to the Bitcoin billionaires club. He was one of the earliest adopters of Bitcoin, starting to early that he remembers seeing just a few computers connected to the designated network. Even though he wasn't as successful as many other Bitcoin investors, he is still a force to be reckoned with. He ended up losing a substantial amount of money in Bitcoins, as a result of hackers' exploits into his mobile and email address top get access to his wallet. Jered did not really tell the public the amount of Bitcoins that were stolen, but he did disclose that he lost millions in dollar value.

Kenna encountered another setback when he lost 800 Bitcoins when his computer was erased in 2010. Not worrying much about the loss as at the time, the hacking feat did brought home a great amount of distress over the money lost. For the fact that Bitcoin doesn't have any provision for transaction reversals, there was no way to retrace and retrieve the money. Despite these odds, Jered Kenna is now a businessman who uses Bitcoins for a large scoop of his transactions. He also encourages the use of the cryptocurrency in business. Even in the face of losses, he was still able to reap the many profits that that helped him grow his business to become what it is today. He now has a large firm which has branches in different countries, and his further investments in cryptocurrency have afforded him the revenue needed to bolster the company's plans for it to become truly multinational. Jered is one of the few people who have had the crypto-shaped monkey on their backs, and still were able to shake it off.

Michael Sloggett

Have you heard of the phrase "Michael Sloggett realizes his dream of building a new home"? If you haven't, meet the owner of the supplements store know n as Second to None in the city of Townsville. Michael Slogget started using digital currencies when he wanted to pay for the supplements he had been getting from international organizations. He was one of the first people to notice and take keen interest in the potential of the currency, after which he started a Bitcoin investment in 2017.

Slogget started out his investments with a $900 sum, and eventually vamped it up to $6,000 by October 2017. With the proceeds from the business, he had enough money to pay off his mortgage and purchased a piece of land in Townsville where he is currently building his new dream home. He started a Facbook page called Crypto Calls, along with five stores in Australia with plans to expand his business through further investments in cryptocurrencies. The larger part of Michael Slogget's seemingly massive wealth has all its roots in digital currencies, and he feels no need to have any worries regarding the future of altcoins.

Erik Finman

Erik Finman is a Bitcoin billionaire who was only 12 years old when his grandmother gave him a sum of $1,000. After some time he decided to invest the entirety of the money in Bitcoin. In 2013, what was a tremendous increase in the monetary value of Bitcoin occurred in the system; a process during which Erik realized that his initial investment had multiplied to $100,000 – which equals 300 Bitcoins. The chap was still in high school as at then, and for his exploits in the cryptocurrency world, he was doing remarkably well for himself already. Seemingly to no one's surprise, he quit school on the backs of his progress so he would have time to found his own company and start making no money – and he did. Starting a company at such age and level in life isn't cakewalk, and no one expects it to be easy. Coupled with the fact that he was investing on something which everyone wasn't really sure of as at then, it was a giant leap on young Erik's part.

Probably as a result of his dropout decision, Finman does not keep it a secret that the current education system is flawed in more ways than one. That is why he went on to establish an organization called Botangle to provide peer-to-peer tutoring services through video chat. In 2015, he found someone who was willing to buy his company; an offer which could have been valued at either $100,000 or 300 Bitcoins. At the time, the cost of the currency was a little less than $200, but Finman decided to take the Bitcoin offer option. His confidence that the digital currency will soon grow paid off in the long run, as her later be4come a millionaire at the age of 18. He is one of the world's youngest crypto-rich businessmen in the space.

giovannicasagrande.com

@ 2018 All rights reserved

www.ingramcontent.com/pod-product-compliance
Lightning Source LLC
Chambersburg PA
CBHW051330220526
45468CB00004B/1571